Faith Ministries, International
Anna C. Bradford
151 Lance Street
Thibodaux, Louisiana 70301
985-665-8476
faithministry07@yahoo.com
annacbradford@gmail.com
facebook.com/faithministry07
http://www.faithministry.vpweb.com

MW01171026

ISBN- 13: 978-1500706319
ISBN- 10:1500706310

Any web addresses or links contained in this book may have changed since publication and may not be valid.

Author makes no claim to its validity but graciously shared the information as it was researched on the internet and given by sources. It is the responsibility of each researcher to establish its accuracy. No sources used in research of this book, including the Author, Publisher, Printer, are responsible for the contents and is free from all litigations.

Some family members chose the rights not to list their husbands or wives if no children were born to them. All family members who were married and had children are listed for the purpose of our children's future generations tracing their ancestors.

WE ARE THE BRANCHES
As A Tree Standing Strong,
In A Place That We Call Home

Anna C. Bradford

Parables Of Life

John 15:5 I am the vine, you are the branches. He that abides in me and I in him, the same brings forth much fruit: For without me you can do nothing.

Dedicated To

To my Lord and Savior, Jesus Christ who saved me from my many sins. The Chaisson Family, past and future. My Father and Mother, William Paul Chaisson Sr. and Elverda Mary Boudreaux Chaisson.

My grandparents and all of my great grandparents. My love extends beyond the memories and the lives of all of my familiy who have gone on to be with the Lord.

As always, I acknowledge my grandchild, Joshua Jordan Bradford, March 30, 2005-March 2007. You are now nine in heaven and someday we will live together in our eternal home with all of our families that have went on before us.

Generational Order "Chaisson"

1. William Paul Chaisson 1927-2009
   Elverda Mary Boudreaux 1929-1996
2. Joseph Arthor Chaisson 1886-1956
   Winona Elizabeth Boudreaux 1898-1937
3. Edwin Henry Clay Chiasson 1857-1921
   Lucinda Eve Gauthier 1858-1939
4. Paul Francois Romain Chiasson 1808-1858
   Marie Bathilde (Rosalia) Bergeron 1815-
5. Francois Joseph Chiasson 1765-After 1808
   Marie Marguerite Lejeune 1769- After 1808
6. Jean Baptiste Chiasson About 1729-After 1785
   Marguerite Josephe Dugas About 1745- Before 1769
7. Francois Chiasson 1697-1759
   Anne Doucet 1703-1758
8. Gabriel (dit Pierre) Chiasson 1667-1741
   Marie Joseph Savoie 1669- Before 1714
9. Guyon (Denis/Dion) Chiasson About 1638-Before 1693
   Jeanne Bernard 1646- Early 1680's
10. Pierre Chiasson About 1614- 1657
    Marie Madeleine Peroche About 1622- After 1638
11. Robert Chiasson 1585-
12. Cyril Chiasson 1560-
    Babara (Connors) Chiasson 1565-

Introduction

"We Are The Branches" A parable in comparison to a Family Tree. A tree standing strong in a place that we call home. A tree planted by the rivers of living water in a place that we know of as life. A family is defined in human context as a group of people affiliated and recognized by birth, by marriage or co residence shared with nature kinship. Life centered around family brings true meaning. Families are so important to God that it was actually recorded many times in the bible. Because of these recordings we know that Jesus was rooted out of the branch of Jesse and the ancestor of David. Genealogy is a field that aims to trace family lineages through history. A family can be used metaphorically to create more categories such as community, global village and nationhood. To fully understand who we really are, we must know where we came from. Families spend time together and learn to know each other. The study of our family's history is the study of our family tree. Trees tend to be long-lived and many of them reaching several thousand years of age. Because of the strength of trees, I have spiritually parabled the tree in reference to our family history standing tall and strong.

With an expansion of twelve generations starting from 1560-2014, I found myself traveling back in time as I located my ancestors one generation at a time.

My ancestors of Acadian, Cajun descendants spread out from West Central France and the Province of New Brunswick, Nova Scotia and Canada. Explore with me into the lives of these ancestors. Many families intertwine in the Chiasson Family Tree through marriages. You might find somewhere along our geneology trail that we are related. We are a family standing strong in a place that we call home.

HISTORY OF THE ACADIANS

Acadians are described as one of the early French settlers of Acadia. Cajun descendant that spoke a dialect of French. Cajun means relating to Acadia or its people, language or culture. Sevententh century French colonist who settled in Acadia. The colony was located in what is now Eastern Canada's Maritime provinces (Nova Scotia, New Brunswick and Prince Edward Island), as well as part of Quebec and presentday Main to the Kennebec River. Today most of the Acadians are French speaking Canadians, Acadia was a seperated colony of New France. Geographically and administratively seperate from the French colony of Canada. The Acadians developed their own history and culture and developed a slightly different French language also.

British Conquest of Acadia in 1710

Acadians lived for almost 80 years in Acadia. After the Conquest, they lived under British rule for the next 45 years. During the French and Indian War, British colonial officers suspected they were aiding the French. The British and New England legislators and militia carried out the Great Expulsion of 1755-1764 during and after the war years. Approximately 11,500 Acadians from the maritime region were departed. Aproximately one-third of the Acadians perished from disease and drowning. Many Acadians migrated to Spanish colonial Luisiana, present day Louisiana state where they developed what became known as Cajun culture. Others were transported to France. Some returned to the provinces of Canada. These were banned from resettling their lands and villages in the land that became Nova Scotia. Most of the Louisiana Cajun descendants now speak English although some still speak Cajun French or a dialect known as Cajun English. The Cajun French dialect was developed in Louisiana. I can remember growing up as a child, GrandMaw and Momma would speak cajun french to each other especially when they did not want us to hear something. Mom said that as a little girl going to school she and the others were forbidden to speak cajun french in school. English was the primary language that the schools insisted on teaching the children.

The Paris French was the language later accepted.

English and its other dialects became predominant only after the Louisiana Purchase when English speaking Americans settled in Louisiana. The name Cajun French derived from the name Colonial French. The Creole Culture includeds French, Spanish, African and Native American cultures. The word came from Portugues and it means crioulo which is a person specifically French descent that was born in the New World. In 1782 Creole was applied to being a salve and a freeman, French, Spanish and Native Americans are identified as Creoles.

Many family names are included in our direct line of Chaisson family tree. Some included are Gautier, Hebert, Boudreaux, Whitney, Lirette, Bergeron, Duplantis, Derocher, Dubois, Crochet, Lancon and Lejeaune. The lineage are strictly on Daddy's side.

God has not cast away his people which he foreknew. Yesterday, today and tomorrow is in the palm of his hands. Life is in his power. He was with our families over five hundred years ago and he is with us today. Tomorrow he will be with our future generation and lead them on into the battles and triumphs of their lives. Today, he upholds our tree and our growing branches as the wind and the storms blow. He straightens our arms when we are weak and when the cares of this world try to snap us away from our tree. Our future family tree is lifted up and rides with God in the wind as he continue to spread our clapping hands in joy. After each cool crisp and sometimes dreary winter he refreshens us with the sweet smelling spring, the building and the planting of vegetables and the planting of flowers and fruits. A new season and a new refreshed life begins.

To my future generation, "Never Give Up, God Is With You". As I write this letter, I am thinking about you long before you were born. I speak to you "You have a purpose and a plan from God and you are loved". "Seek God"
This is my gift to you. One day you may be interested in knowing your family tree and where you came from. This is the knowledge of your generations and of your ancestors. It is shared for you and for all of the world.

Join me now as we begin our long journey into the lives of many ancestors. The trials and triumphs of each generation branching out and creating our gigantic tree of life. Seasons of rain, windstorms and hurricanes shake our branches to a near breaking. The incredible journey of our roots lead us into a spiritual parable of life in comparison to a Family Tree and "We Are The Branches".

Chapter 1

A Tree Standing Strong

Generation 1
1927-2009
William Paul Chaisson Sr. 11/26/1929-4/3/2009
Elverday Mary Boudreaux 11/14/1927-12/5/1996

As our generational tree stand silently in the background of my existence, the desire to know my family has been exposed in a way that I had never begun to imagine. I suddenly found myself longing to know more about my ancestors. A sort of heritditary perennial plant supported by our branches, standing strong in a place that I came to know of as home. If home is where the heart is then family is where love is. Nurtured by my family trunk that contained unimaginable strength, our axis rotated and God determined the direction of our lives. I dreamt of a time that I could search and would find any extension of my family. Where they came from? What kind of life they had? My family tree had been preserved from all of the outside elements by the layers of bark that had been protecting it long ago. Today, it stands strong in the midst of a forest. As each generation grew, we withstood the shadows of our existence and the tests of our times. From under the ground, our healthy roots spread out as sweet breaths of life pouring out onto us. Our roots anchored down and it fed our family tree and our branches, nurturing us with the fullness of our being. We awakened from the darkest surface as my faith brought us out into the marvelous light. Our family buds soon branched out above ground forming shoots that bear many of our leaves today. Our family tree has proven to be long-lived from generation to generation. Daily providing us with shade and shelter for the days that we become weary. Providing us with peace when we endure heartaches. Providing delicious fruit for the picking when we become hungry. Our family tree is a solid and secure tree standing strong in a place of existence that I have come to know of as our loving home. Our tree of knowledge, wisdom and love stands gracefully and seeks out who we really are.

Together, let us set out on a long journey into many generations of past families living long ago. Although the lives of these incredible people are no longer walking this earth today, I gain strength from the wisdom and knowledge that I received from them. I take that wisdom and knowledge, spread it abroad like the bark of our tree and use it as mulch. Protecting and surrounding our family tree with colorful leaves as they softly touch the ground. For many years I have researched my family roots because of curiosity and a hearts desire to know who they are and acknowledge where I came from. It is my hearts desire that this book will spark an interest in you to find, study and research your own family out. In doing this I gained knowledge, strength and courage and I pray that you will also. Since our Cajun heritage came from off of the ships to populate the areas of Louisiana there are many of us who are related and do not realize it. It is with great joy and a priviledge to introduce to you my family starting with the youngest generation, my Father.

William (Bill) Paul Chaisson was born on November 26, 1927. Bill had five brothers total, William, Linward, Joseph (J.C.), Bobbie and Charles Chaisson. Charles was deceased at a young age. One sister named Marjorie Chaisson who was deceased at a very young age. The story was told that she tragically died of accidental poisoning after she swallowed washing detergent. Bill and Elverda had fourteen children. Elverda miscarried one of her children leaving a total of seven boys and six girls. The seven boys are Charles Joseph Chaisson, named after Daddy's brother). Daddy's deceased brother meant so much to him that he would recognize him by naming his first born after him. Charles married Nancy Guidry and together they had Monica Ann, Travis and Thomas Chaisson. Monica was my first niece and my Father and Mother's first grand child. William Paul Jr. (named after Daddy) married Rita Cloutre, William and Rita had Melissa Ann and William Paul Chaisson the third. Melissa has twins, Joselynn and Jaselynn. Both Charles and William served in the Viet Nam War about 1968-1971. Charles in Viet Nam and William served in Germany. I am very proud of my brothers for serving their country and risking their lives for the freedom we have today. William Jr. died tragically in a car wreck on July 11, 1998, two years after our Mother passed away. We were all sadened that our second brother left this earth when he was forty-nine years of age. It is so hard when someone you know and love unexpectly dies. A void and hurt that never goes away. Chester Michael, married to Sandra. Chester had one daughter, Tammy from a previous relationship. Chester died after complications from a gun shot wound to his chest by his previous relationship. Another tragedy that left us devastated. Sheila Ann married Robert Theriot and they had Robert Jr. and

William Paul. Patricia Marie married Edmund Daniel Fallon and they had Troy, Christopher and Shannon Fallon. Marjorie Ann, named after Daddy's sister, married Kirby Rivere and they had Shane Paul and Dawn Marie Rivere. Autry John married Maria Davidson and they have Jodi, Starleigh and Benjamin. He married again Brenda Evans and they had Taylor and Tyler Chaisson. Wenona Elizabeth, named after Grand Maw Winona Chaisson, married Curtis Lirette and they had Bridgett, Sunshine, Curtis Jr. and Seth. Carlton James married Karen and they had Corey and Carlton Jr. Angela Mary married Keith Richard and later married Jodi Young and they have Amanda and Joshua Young. She is now married to Billy Maronge. Anna Marie married Michael Bradford and we have Michael Jr., Nicholas Roy and Jordan Paul Bradford. Timothy Calvin was never married and Joseph Author Chaisson, named after our Grand Paw Joe, married Colette Ann Voisin and they had Brittany Lynn, Skylar Rene and Joseph Author Chaisson Jr. (Jo Jo) who by the way loves to read books and loves Art. Joseph was born on November 13, 1962 and he was the thirteenth living child.

After the death of Bill's Mom, Winona Boudreaux Chaisson at the age of nine and a half, Bill was placed in an all boys school in New Orleans, Louisiana. Bill's Father, Paw Paw Joe was not able to continue taking care of the family. In those days most of the women took care of the children and the household. The men worked mostly outside and provided for their family. Most of the men knew nothing at all about taking care of children. Winona had been sick with Pluricy and she passed on at the early age of 39. Paw Paw Joe was not able to take care of the children so he regretfully gave them up to live in an orphanage. Living in the all boys home was rough for Daddy. Catholic nuns with strict upbringing was forced upon him. This type of raising caused him to be skeptical about his religious background and later shyed away from the church. The lack of the show of love from his surroundings caused him to hide his feelings and emotions.

At the age of almost nineteen, Bill married Elverda. Elverda was almost seventen years of age when she married Bill in Terrebonne Parish, Houma, Louisiana. Elverda met Bill when a friend bet her that she would not whistle at this young man walking down the street. She did and they met and married and the rest was literally history.

Almost thirteen years after they were married, I was born. Dad was almost thirty two years of age when I was born and Mom was almost twenty nine. So young to have had eleven children at the age of twenty nine. Yet she lived for all of her children constantly denying her own self. A denyal that would too soon come back to haunt her.

Mom died of complications following a heart attack on Thursday, December 5, 1996 at the age of sixty-seven. She was very sickly with high blood pressure and she was a diebetic with an enlarged heart that eventually caused the heart attack. When I was sixteen years of age one of my Mohter's legs was amputated because of blood clots due to a blood disease and possibly birth control pills. Charles and Marjorie inherited that blood disorder and Marjorie passed it on to her children Shane and Dawn. Shane almost died when blood clots passed through his heart. Later Marjorie had blood clots form and passed through her lungs. God spared the both of them for they lived through this.

Dad died on Friday, April 3, 2009 at 7:00 am in Terrebonne Parish, Houma, Louisiana at the age of eighty-two after he battled years of Alzheimer's disease. He lost his cognitive ability over a period of years. Daddy was a hard working man, very strong and independent. He taught me many things about life and that life does not owe us anything. We come into this life with many expectations. Life does not always meet those expectations. Daddy was stripped away from his Mother at nine years of age. His life took a dramatic change when he became a refuge with other orphaned boys and impoverished families. Living at Hope Haven, founded by Monsignor Peter Wynhoven in 1925, was not always easy. His brothers resided at Madonna Manor, a home for younger boys and girls near Hope Haven. The story Daddy told us were of harsh and brutal conditions. There were no rules and regulations on how to treat children back then. Social Services were not involved in any events that happened. Basically, teachers were enforcers and could really do what ever they needed to do to enforce discipline. They were correctors and took matters into their own hands. Daddy's surroundings were hardly ever pleasant. He was not shown the love and nurture that he needed as a child. After Maw Maw Winona died love was not taught to him therefore love was hard for him to show. He had complications showing love even though we knew that he loved us. He was tempermental at times but we always knew that he loved us. I never needed to hear it because I almost always felt his love.

Recently the Archdiocese of New Orleans announced that it was shutting down the children's treatment facility after more than eighty years of service. Many boys later filed suits claiming of abuse, neglect and molestation. Some of the boys claimed that they were put into a closet for days and were beaten repeatedly and abused. Daddy never told us the whole story of what happened but he did say that he was treated with abuse by the nuns. This had a horrible impact upon his life. He later rejected church and never wanted to step foot into a church. His bitterness grew also for his Father. He found real love when he married Elverda. Elverda was so patient and had compassion for others. She certainly had enough love to shed abroad. Momma loved the Lord and would pray daily. She was a peace maker and a home maker. I learned so much virtue from her. Before Momma and Daddy died they confessed Jesus into their lives and I was greatful for this. I always knew they loved the Lord but hearing them speak it was comforting to me.

For the law of Spirit of life in Christ Jesus hath made me free from the law of sin and death. There is good and bad in this life. We can not call good bad nor bad good. We have to scope out the good and do good, get rid of the bad and be blessed. There was so much bad done to Daddy but he stayed strong as a tree wavering in the storms. His strength pouring down as a faucet onto us. Proving to us that this tree could live longer than any other human being. Its branches were going to stretch out to an unbelievable height, width and depth. His branches were not going to be thrown in the fire. His life was not going to be lived in vain. Sometimes we get so wrapped up and consumed in life that we forget to live. When we slow down we breathe life.

The old oak tree still stands near by where our house once sat. The house is no longer there where Daddy and Mamma made us a home but the tree still stands strong. The tree representing strength and the symbol of love as life poured down on our family. Although it stands alone physically, it stands spiritually in the wilderness on the side of the forest of trees. Our tree stands upright as the strength of our family background stands tall and straight. Daddy represented a tree standing strong in a place that we call home. His life stood as a pillar that would not fall. A strong representation of our family tree and we are the branches.

Chapter 2

We Are The Branches

Generation 2
1886-1956
Joseph Arthor Chaisson 12/28/1886-11/28/1956
Winona Elizabeth Boudreaux Chaisson 03/28,1898-
4/7/1937

As the acknowledgement of our family began to branch out, clutsters of limbs began to sprout out from our tree. Strength and growth widened and expanded from the strong trunk of our living family tree. I was excited to find out more information and shed a light on what once was my darkened, shadowed past. Who were they? Where did they live? What were their lives like? All of these questions had been brewing inside of me for a long time. These questions began to birth new answers.

Joseph Arthor Chaisson was born in Terrebonne Parish on December 28, 1886. Winona was also born in Terrebonne Parish on March 28, 1898 just before the turn of the century. Joseph was almost twelve years older than Winona. When Joseph was about thirty years of age he married Winona who was eighteen years of age. They were married in Terrebonne Parish. Eleven years after they were married Daddy was born. Together they had five sons and one daughter. After twenty-one years of marriage to Joseph, Winona died of Pluricy on April 7, 1937. Daddy was just nine years of age when his Mom, Winona was deceased. Joseph died nineteen years after his wife died and exactly one month before his seventyth birthday in Terrebonne Parish, Houma, Louisiana. I had just turned three years old when Paw Paw Joe died. I do not remember Paw Paw Joe but I often hear stories about him from my family. When he died silver coins were placed in his eyes.

I keep a picture in a frame on the wall of him, Maw Maw Winona and Great Grandmaw Eva. A huge tree stood standing strong in the back of them. How ironic, "A Family Tree". To everything there is a reason. Look for the reason. A tree planted near the streams of living water where its roots bring forth life. Faith, hope and love were the roots brought forth the tree of life to our family.

Ezekiel 117:5-10 He took also of the seed of the land and planted it in the fruitful field. He placed it by great waters and set it as a willow tree. And it grew and became a spreading vine of low stature, whose branches turned toward him and the roots therof were under him: so it became a vine and brought forth branches and shot forth sprigs. There were also another great eagle with great wings and many feathers: and, behold, this vine did bend her roots toward him and shot forth her branches toward him that he might water it by the furrows of her plantation. It was planted in a good soil by great waters that it might be a godly vine. Say thou, Thus saith the Lord God; Shall it prosper? Shall he not pull up the roots therof and cut off the fruit thereof that it wither? It shall wither in all the leaves of her spring even without great power of many people to pluck it up by the roots thereof. Yea, behold, being planted, shall it prosper? Shall it not utterly wither when the east wind touches it? It shall wither in the furrows where it grew. What God plants, it grows and prospers. Although it withers, strength upholds our family tree. Although we become weary, we are held in his arms. God is the vine and we are the branches. We are a limb growing from the trunk of the divine tree of life. We come forth as a branch spreading and shooting out from all sides. Life in the vine is nurturing us and sending us forth. Without the vine we can do nothing. He is the foundation, the ground of our roots. We will not be uprooted because God is the anchor of our roots. We are the branches, rooted and grounded in love. God is love so we are rooted and grounded in God.

Ephesians 3:13-21 (13)Wherefore I desire that you faint not at my tribulations for you, which is your glory.

Jesus paid the price for us in sorrows and tribulations just for us. If you were the only person left on this earth, Christ would have died for you. That is our glory to him as a servant of God. (14) For this cause I bow my knees unto the Father of our Lord Jesus Christ, (15) Of whom the whole family in heaven and earth is named, (16) That he would grant you, according to the riches of his glory, to be strengthened with might by his Spirit in the inner man; (17) That Christ may dwell in your hearts by faith; that you, being rooted and grounded in love, (18) May be able to comprehend with all saints what is the breadth and length and depth and height; (19) And to know the love of Christ, which passes knowledge, that you might be filled with all the fullness of God. (20) Now unto him that is able to do exceeding abundantly above all that we ask or think, in us, (21) Unto him be glory in the church by Christ Jesus throughout all ages, world without end. Amen!

We are the branches and the anchor of our roots is Love. We are rooted and grounded in God, who is love. His love toward us is shed abroad for all the world to see so that they know we are Christians by this love.

Chapter 3

The Anchor, Our Roots

Generation 3
1857-1939
Edwin Henry Clay Chiasson 05/13/1857-6/7/1921
Lucinda Eve Gauthier Chiasson 10/30/1858-1939

The anchor which is our roots planted deep under the ground holds our family tree stable and upright. A tree never has to worry whether it will grow or not. We do not ever have to worry if we will grow because the anchor, which is our roots, holds us in place. The spiritual roots of our family tree forseen long ago that as we were but only a seed, we would need to spend time planted under the ground and in the darkness. As we spent time in the darkness we would be brought forth into light and know how to live in that light. Darkness is a part of life. When God created the world he seperated the darkness and the light. Light became day and darkness became night. We all must face darkness while we live here on this earth. We all will face trials and tribulations in our lives in order for us to grow and mature. It defines our character and identity. God has created each of us and has uniquely designed us exactly as he sees us. Although our roots stay underground and lack the fullness of light and life, our roots spread abroad traveling into the world as we choose to bring light or darkness. Roots are never exposed yet they are the most significant part of the tree. It serves as the support part. It stores food, water and other minerals from soil. Our roots firmly establish us and spread across boundaries as we live our lives. Our healthy roots supply vital nurishment that our family tree need to expand and to grow. We all must create sound and rooted boundaries in our lives that we can not cross over. Morality should never cross over immorality. Incorruptible should never intertwine into corruptible. If we allow ourselves to set our feet over the boundary lines and make inmature mistakes we become immoral, think irrational and live corruptible. We then become a bad seed living an unhealthy life style. Whatsoever a man sows that he shall also reap. When we sow bad seeds, we will reap them also. We must live life sowing good seeds at whatever cost. Goodness will prevail no matter how bad life seems.

Romans 11:162-24(16) For if the first fruit be holy, the lump is alos holy: and if the root be holy, so are the branches. Clean and holy roots sprout out clean and holy branches but unclean roots sprout out unclean branches. (17) And if some of the branches be broken off, and thou, being a wild olive tree, were graffed in among them, and with them partakest of the root and fatness of the olive tree; (18) Boast not against the branches. but if thou boast, thou bearest not the root, but the root thee. (19) Thou will say then, The branches were broken off, that I might be grafted in. (20) Well; because of unbelief they were broken off, and thou stand by faith. Be not highminded, but fear: (21) For if God spared not the natural branches, take heed lest he also spare not thee. (22) Behold therefore the goodness and severity; but toward thee, goodness, if thou continue in his goodness: otherwise thou also shall be cut off. (23) And they also, if they abide not still in unbelief, shall be graffed in: for God is able to graff them in again.(24) For if thou were cut out of the olive tree which is wild by nature, and were graffed contrary to nature into a good olive tree: how much more shall these, which be the natural branches be graffed inot their own olive tree? By Jesus sparing us, we were cut out of our sin nature and graffed into the vine (Jesus). If we continue into his goodness we shall continue to be a holy branch. If we do not continue in his goodness than we shall be cut off.

Everyone has ancestor roots and today with many resources and new technology we can locate them easier than we have ever done before. If you know a few of your ancestors birth dates or death dates then you can start to locate your own family tree. In search of your roots to your branches you will find your "God created Family Tree".

Our first Great Grand Father, Edwin Henry Clay Chiasson was born on May 13, 1857 in Houma, Louisiana. Louisiana is the only state in the United States where we have parishes instead of counties. This stems from the Catholic Church when the community people were called parishiners. Houma, Louisiana is part of Terrebonne Parish. Edwin was baptised at St. Francis Church in Terrebonne Parish in Houma, Louisiana. He married Lucinda Gautier, also known as Gauthier, on July 5, 1876 at the age of nineteen in Terrebonne Parish, Houma, Louisiana. Together they had Henry George Chiasson, born March 15, 1881 in Houma, Louisiana. Cara Josephine, Emelie Chiasson. Faye Marie Chiasson, July 22, 1890. Ema Venice Chiasson, born Sept. 5, 1893 in Terrebonne Parish, Houma, Louisiana. Paul Nolton Chiasson born September 11, 1899 and Clifford Cleophes, born December 27,1884. They all were babtised in St. Francis Church in Houma, Louisiana. Lucinda was born on

October 30, 1858 in Terrebonne Parish. She was a very strong woman. There was an article in the paper with her and one of her daughters. It was published on April of 2007 where she is seen pouring coffee for her daughter. Great Grand Father Edwin had already passed away and Lucinda was a widow at the time. The article was about their daughter who married a son of a confederate soldier, that was a conscript. He was captured after the fall of Vicksburg. Her daughter's Father in law, Ulysse Jean Baptiste Bergeron refused to sign parole paper and spent over a year as a prisoner of war. I am so blessed to have pictures of my Great Grand Mothers, Grand Mother, Grand Father and one of my Great Aunts.

Our Great Grand Father, Edwin was a laborer. He did unskilled physical work that was very productive and difficult. It was very exhausting work. He was born one hundred two years and four months before I was born. Edwin died June 7, 1921 almost one month of his sixty-fourth birthday. Lucinda died in 1939 at approximately eighty-one years old, barely two years after Daddy's Mother, Maw Maw Winona passed away. Lucinda outlived Edwin Henry by eighteen years. Daddy was barely twelve years old when Lucinda, his Grand Mother passed away making it impossible to live with them. Edwin Henry Clay died before Daddy was born by about six years.
No one knows why the spelling of the Chiasson name was changed from Chiasson to Chaisson. The generation of my Grand Father Joseph Arthur Chaisson changed the spelling. Uncle J.C., Daddy's brother, was the only brother who kept the Chiasson spelling. Possibly a birth certificate error.
Edwin is buried in St. Francis Cemetarty in Houma, Louisiana. Lucinda died in 1939. This Chiasson generation lasted from

1857-1939. Over one century was covered since I set out on a long journey to locate my ancestors. Exactly one hundred years after my Great Grand Father was born, I came into this world. Our blood line was traveling through history and through time. Our generational tree was on a course and it was reaching its destination. God's perfect plan was unfolding and I was one step closer to finding our families destiny.

Chapter 4

The Destination Of Our Family Tree

Generation 4
1808-1858
Paul Francois Romain Chiasson 01/26/1808-1858
Bathilde Marie(Rosalie) Bergeron Chiasson 05/15/1815-

The trunk of our family tree determined the direction that our family tree would go in. The trunk of a tree has the same job as the head does for the body. It turns the whole tree and places it in the direction that it needs to go in. Our family tree was on a course and a direction that God had planted long before we all were ever born.

The trunk of a tree is defined as the main woody axis of a tree. The shaft of a column. Axis is a line on which something rotates on or evenly arranged. It determines the left and the right sides. It is the main stem of the plant. In the book of Jeremiah, God had a plan for us and for our lives. The plan was never to harm us but to give us a future and a hope. That was always the plan of God. His intentions were never to hurt us but to love us with an unconditional love. His guidance and direction was always simple and less complicated yet we choose to include the things in our lives that are more complicated. His vision for our lives is to stand tall as a strong tree. When all we have done is to stand, we will stand. Strength and honor is born when we take heed, unless we fall. He has ordained us to go forth and be a blessing to all of the world.

James 3:10-18 (10) Out of the same mouth proceeds blessings and cursing. My brethren, these things ought not so to be. (11) Does a fountain send forth at the same place sweet water and bitter? (12) Can the fig tree, my brethren bear olive berries? either a vine, figs? so can no fountain both yield salt water and fresh. (13) Who is a wise man and endued with knowledge among you? Let him shew out of a good conversation his works with meekness and wisdom. (14) But if you have bitter, envying and strife in your hearts, glory not and lie not against the truth. (15) This wisdom descendes not from above but is eathly, sensual and devilish. (16) For where envying and strife is, there is confusion and every evil work. (17) But the wisom that is from above is first pure, then peaceable, gentle and easy to be intreated, full of mercy and good fruits, without partiality and without hyposcrisy. (18) And the fruit of righteousness is sown in peace of them that make peace. Peace makers are of fresh water and not salt water. Jealousy is of an evil seed and a part of the dead sea.

Our destination lies within us. We all were placed on this earth for a season and a speck of time. What we do with our time while we are in our body determines our eternal destination. Jesus bore our sins in his own flesh when his body was on "The Tree". We were dead in our sins but now live unto righteousness because of what he did on that tree. Each stripe he endured healed us from physical, mental and spiritual anguish. Clouds we were without water, carried about in every wind. We were fruitless trees, plucked up by our roots. Our lives traveled meaningless down a path of no return without him. We can do nothing without Christ. When we think we are strong in our own ways we are deceived by the enemy. Our tree is cut down and our branches are cast into the fire. Our strength comes from the Lord. He has carried my family from generation to generation. We must acknowledge him as our Lord!

Our second Great Grand Father, Paul was also known as Hypolite Paul. He is our second great grandfather on my Fathers side. Born on January 26, 1808 in Donaldsonvile, Ascension Parish in Louisiana. He was christened on August 22, 1808 in Donaldsonville at an Ascension Church in Louisiana. Paul resided in Terrebonne Parish. He married Bathilde Marie (Rosalie) Bergeron on May 3, 1830 in Terrebonne Parish, Louisiana. He was aproximately 22 years of age. Rosalie was born on May 15, 1815 in Plattenville, Louisiana. She married Paul twelve days after her fiftenth birthday. Paul was about seven years older than Rosalie. It was not uncommon for a younger girl to marry an older man. Most young women did marry early in life. They knew their role as a married women would be to take care of their children and the household. Yet Paul's occupation is listed as a Housekeeper. A housekeeper is defined as one who is employed to perform or direct the domestic tasks in a household. Also known as a house husband or housewife.

This generation is relatable to me because together, Paul and Rosalie had thirteen children. My Daddy and Mom had thirteen children also. One of their children was Edwin Henry Clay Chiasson who carried our blood line and family tree. Henry Clay was born the eleventh child and I am the eleventh child of my family also. Between the seventh and eighth child, they moved from Thibodaux, Lafourche Parish to Houma, Terrebonne Parish. The next generations all resided in Terrebonne Parish,

Houma, Louisiana. A city about sixty miles south of New Orleans, Louisiana where their ancestors arrived on the ships from France, Nova Scotia and Canada. Paul set a course for the next generations to plant their feet in a parish that I came to know of as home. I was born and raised in Terrebonne Parish, Houma, Lousiana. I grew up on a plantation called South Coast. Sugar cane was planted and harvested in the area that my family grew up at. My Father and Mother raised thirteen children down on this plantation. Daddy worked for South Coast Corporation for thirty-three years and made a living working hard. Our feet was planted on solid ground and the destination of our family tree had been planted into existence long ago. This generation set the course and the road that our family would take us on for many generations. Bayou Dularge, a fishing, trawling and trapping community about eight miles outside of Houma would be the grounds that my feet would be planted on for many years to come.

Chapter 5
Protected Underneath The Shadow

Generation 5
1765-
Francois Joseph Chaisson (Joseph Francis Chiasson)
11/10/1765-After 1808
Marie Simoneaux 1767-After 12/30 1795
Marie Marguerite Lejeune 8/14/1769-After 1808

As our "Family Tree" is revealed one generation at a time, I am fascinated at how I perceive my family and how they are slowly revealing themselves to me. As if we were spreading the wings of God and taking on a new flight. Sheltered by his wings as we continued to live in peace and harmony. As my research continues, I am constantly reminded of Revelation 22:2 In the midst of the street of it, and on either side of the river, was there the tree of life, which bare twelve manner of fruits, and yielded her fruit every month: and the leaves of the tree were for the healing of the nations. God had a plan all along for our family. Our leaves on our tree was spreading for the nations. The things we were about to endure would be healing for the nation. Our roots and upward layers of stems were revealing itself to me. My eyes were beginning to open up and life was teaching me the things that I needed to find out. The spiritual bark of our tree was in plain view and had come to life. The outermost layers of stems and roots of our Family Tree was protected by its bark. As mulch spread abroad across the lands, our colorful landscape became attractive in the eyes of those that followed us. As our family spread its wings, we were hidden in the shadow of the almighty God. Safe and protected from the elements of this life. Our tree found refuge and strength. We set out on a long and intense journey with a sense of belonging in a place that accepted us as our ancestors began a new life in a new world that they knew nothing of. United States, home of the free and the land of the brave. A country that accepts every culture and every background regardless of their color, gender or religion. When we were rejected because of our culture and Cajun French dialect, South Louisiana, accepted our ancestors for who we were. We were forbidden to speak our language by the Englanders. Cajun French was considered the poor man french therefore it was banned from us. We were a culture that society hated and rejected. A sense that my ancestor's only desire was to be accepted and not rejected or departed. I soon sensed the outcast and start to feel the compatable relation to the African Americans as they were sold into slavery. I come to realize that the only way we would survive in this cruel, harsh world would be by the Grace of God. His protection underneath the shadow of his wings. My heart grieved at each heart break findings. As I gained closer ground and step into another branch of my Acadian, Cajun family.

Our third Great Grand Father, Francois Joseph Chiasson was born on November 10, 1765 in France. When Joseph was nineteen years of age he boarded the ship L'Amitie from France to Louisiana along side of his Father Jean Baptiste Chiasson and and his Father's third wife, Anne (Joanne). His half brother Pierre who was fifteen and was born around 1761 was also on that ship. Great Grand Father Joseph was a ropemaker and his Dad was a carpenter. Together they probably were used on the ship as workers.

After the ship landed in New Orleans, Louisiana in 1785, Joseph and his parents and half brother, Pierre found refuge in Plattenville, Assumption Parish, Louisina. Almost four years later, Joseph married Marie Simoneaux on July 17, 1789 in Plattenville, Louisiana. Joseph was twenty-three and a half years of age and Marie was about twenty-two. They birthed four children all in Planttenville, Louisiana. The first born was Francois Victor Chiasson born on August 6, 1790. Their second born was Pierre Alexandre Chiasson born on August 18, 1793. Their twins, Isabelle and Marcelin Joseph Chiasson were born on December 30, 1795.

Two years later Joseph married his second wife, Marie Marguerite Lejeune on January 7, 1797 in Assumption Parish, Louisiana. There is no report of the death date of both Marie Simoneaux and Joseph. Joseph's first wife, Marie died while giving birth to the twins at the age of about twenty-nine in Plattenville, Louisiana according to other researches.

Twelve years after Joseph boarded the Ship L'Amitie, Joseph married his second wife Marie Marguerite Lejeune, born on August 14, 1769. Together they had four children also. Lucie Carmelite was born July 30, 1798, around one year and six months after they were married. Their second child, Jean Baptiste Prudent Chiasson was born on June 25, 1800. Their third child, Florentine Bernard Joseph was born on August 15, 1804. Their fourth child was the youngest of their children, Paul Francois Romain Chiasson, our blood line and my direct family tree line, was born on January 26, 1808. Joseph was almost thirty-two years of age and Marie was twenty-eight when they married. Joseph married his second wife seven and a half years after he married his first wife. Both marriages were in Louisiana, Assumption Parish and Plattenville, Louisiana, about four years after his voyage from France to Louisiana with his Father, Mother and brother.

Marie Marguerite Lejeune was sixteen years of age when she boarded the Le Saint Remi Ship from France to Louisiana. She immigrated with her widowed Mother, Anastasie Levron who was born on October 29, 1737 in Port Royal, Acadia. Her Father Amand Lejeune was born in Acadia in 1727. Amand died, one year before his widow set sail, in Nantes, France at the age of about fifty-seven. Anastasie Levron was forty-five years of age upon the ship. She and her six children, two sons and four daughters, were aboard together. Joseph Lejeune was a sailor and was twenty-two years of age. Alexis was a son and was thirteen years of age. Marie Rose was eighteen years of age. Marguerite was sixteen years of age. Magdelaine was six years of age and Rosalie was two years of age. Anastasie never remarried. She died in Lafourche Parish on November of 1823 at eighty-six years of age.

The French ship Saint Remi was a four hundred ton ship. On June 27, 1785 it left Nantes, France. The commander was Captain Baudin. Three hundred and twenty-five Acadians and sixteen stowaways were on that ship when it departed from France to New Orleans, Louisiana. On September 10, 1785 it arrived in New Orleans. Fifteen passengers perished during the voyage. Marie Marguerite Lejeune was not one of them because she married Francois Joseph Chaisson, my fourth Great Grand Father, on January 7, 1797 in Assumption Parish, Louisiana.

Chapter 6

New Lands, New Boundaries

Generation 6
1729-
Jean Baptiste Chiasson 1729-After 1785
Marriage 1 Louise Marguerite (Pretieux) 8/29/1734
Marriage 2 Marguerite Josephe Dugas About 1738
Marriage 3 Anne Perrine (Joanne) Chiasson About 1745

When our fourth Great Grand Father aboarded the ship The
L'Amitie, I'm sure he had a lot on his mind. Coming to a strange
land with his third wife, Anne (Joanne) and their fifteen year old
son, Pierre and Jean's previous marriage son, my blood line,
Francois Joseph Chiasson. Being on the ship with some of his
family would be a challenge. A new life lies ahead of him like
buds opening up for the first time. Undeveloped land to
cultivate, leafy shoots sprouting out and spreading over harsh
conditions. His first stage of a different kind of life. A life of
freedom was anticipated and forseen. Dreams and thoughts
about clearing the land and making a new home for his family
were about to become a reality.

Leaving the old life behind would probably be no challenge for
them because the Acadians were outcasted. Spain invited the

Acadians to settle in Louisiana to populate the area. An opportunity for a new beginning was on our horizon. Acadians were known as hard working people and they were self sufficient. They built their own houses and what they did not build with their own hands they bartered with the Englanders even though it was against the law at that time. They were known as God fearing people who had strength to minister to others. They were a great example to the community because of their faith. Research has proven that my ancestors were of the faith and were good shepherds, leaders. They took care of their family and their people. They were considered and kind to all and had a peace making spirit. Acadians, Cajun French people were very friendly and had little trouble making friends. At times they were too kind which led them to be used and abused. Their kindness at times was also mistaken as weakness.

Jean Baptiste Chiasson was born on about 1729. He was my fourth Great Grandfather. He was the son of Francois Chiasson born in 1697 in Beaubassin, Acadia and Anne Doucet born in 1703 in Port Royal, Acadia.
When Jean was about twenty-three years of age he married his first wife, Louise Marguerite (Pretieux) Precieux about the year of 1752. Louise was born on August 29, 1734 in the Isle of St. Jean, Acadia. She was about eighteen years of age when she married Jean. There is no research found on whether Jean and Louise had any children.

Aproximately nine years later, Jean married his second wife, Marguerite Josephe Dugas on June 30, 1761 in Ondes, Ille et Vilaine at St. Melior Church in Canada. Jean was around thirty-two and Marguerite was about twenty-three years of age.

Marguerite was my fourth Great Grandmother. She and Jean had two known children. Jean Baptiste Chiasson Jr. who was born on January 27, 1763 in La Blanche, Ille et Vilaine, France and Francois Joseph Chiasson. Francois Joseph was born on November 10, 1765 and he was my direct blood line and family descendant. His Father Jean was about thirty-six years of age when Francois was born. His Mother Marguerite was around twenty-seven years of age.

Jean's third wife was Anne Perrine (Joanne) who was born in about 1745. Joanne was around 24 when they married on January 10, 1769. Jean and Joanne had a child, Pierre Chaisson born around 1770. On August 20, 1785, they sailed on the ship The L'Amitie and landed in New Orleans, Louisiana on November 8, 1785. Our familiy settled along Bayou Lafourche and its surrounding areas. The name Lafourche comes from the French word meaning "fork", because of the bayou's large outflow of the Mississippi River water. The first settlements of Acadians in South Louisiana lived near Bayou Lafourche and Bayou des Ecores, these two closely associated. The bayou is known as Cajun culture. Acadians, Cajuns settled and made a family down many of the bayous of Louisiana. Research proves that my family settled all along Bayou Lafourche and spreading out unto other bayous. Bayou Dularge was one of the bayous that my Father and Mother chose to settle down and raise a family. The bayous are from a Mississippi outlet but was later dammed up at Donaldsonville in 1905. This caused a lack of nourishment in the wetland areas of central Louisiana changing the natural flowing bayou into a stagnant dead ditch.

The Lafourche des Chetimachas River is a fork that is 106 mile long bayou in southeastern Louisiana. It flows into the Gulf of Mexico. This bayou is known as the longest Main Street in the world. It runs between Louisiana Highway 1 on the west and Louisiana Highway 308 on the east. It flows through parts of Ascension, Assumption and Lafourche parishes. Today, approximately 300,000 Louisiana residents drink water from the bayou according to research.

Here in the United States, on July 4, 1776, the colonies were fighting Great Brittain in what is known as the American Revolutionary War. The Declaration of Independence was issued by the delegates from the thirteen colonies. The war ended in 1783 and the United States was an independent country. We were now seperated from Great Brittain, a war of independence against a European colonial empire. In 1787, the Constitution was adopted. Then came the Bill of Rights.

On April 30, 1812, Louisiana was admitted to the Union as the eightenth state. Union, Justice and Confidence became our motto. Our officicial language was Spanish, French and English. The Bayou State, Sportsman's Paradise, The Pelican State, The Sugar State, and The Creole State were some of the names that were established for Louisiana. Before the American purchase of the territory in 1803, Louisiana had been Spanish and French colony. The development also included importing African slaves in the eightenth century. Louisiana has more native tribes than any other state. Baton Rouge is the capital of the state and New Orleans is the largest city in Louisiana.

Jean Baptiste Chiasson, his wife, Anne (Joanne), Jean's son from his second marriage to Marguerite, Joseph (Francois) Chaisson and his son with Joanne, Pierre Chiasson were all passengers and boarded the ship called L'Amitie. In French it means friendship. Jean was fifty-six years of age. Joanne was forty years of age. Joseph Chiasson, a ropemker and my third Great Grand Father, was nineteen years of age and Pierre Chiasson was fifteen years of age when they all boarded the ship. Led by Captain Joseph Beitremieux, they left France on August 20, 1785. They sailed the dangerous tumultrous waters for eighty days. They arrived in New Orleans, Louisiana on November 8, 1785. There were 8 families and a total of 270 people on the ship. Sickness and diseases spread abroad the ship and there were six deaths. Seventy-one families chose to settle along Bayou Lafourche. My ancestors have become known as "Cajuns". The L'Amite was the fifth out of seven ships involved in the exodus of Acadians from France to Louisiana in 1785. They departed Nantes, France and arrived in New Orleans almost three months later. Louisiana was a Spanish colony at that time. The Spanish name for the fifth ship was called the La Amistad when it arrived. Spain invited the Acadians to come and settle in Louisiana to populate the areas. They paid for the seven ships to come from France to Louisiana. The opportunity for a new beginning and to join some of our kin that had already been here was something that they could not pass up. One third of Acadians came to Lousiana. One third stayed in France and one third of the people chose Novia Scotia. Jean was fifty-six years of age when he was a passenger on the ship L'Amite. Anne (Joanne) was forty years of age. His son, Joseph Chiasson was a rope maker and was nineteen on the ship. Pierre was fifteen years of age. Jean, and his wife, aboarded the L'Amitie which departed from Painbouef, France on August 12, 1785. It arrived in New Orleans, Louisiana approximately on November 8, 1785. On December 1785, they were moved by boat to Valenzuel which was a place near Donaldsonville, Louisiana.

Seven Ships Sailed From France To Louisiana

Le Bon Papa: During the 1785 excile, the first ship that left France on Tuesday, May 10, 1785. The ship arrived in Louisiana on July 29, 1785. It spent 80 days at sea. 36 families,156 people on board. one child died on trip.

La Berger: The second ship to leave France on June 11, 1785 and arrived in Louisiana on August 15, 1785 after 93 days at sea.

Le Beaumont: The third ship left on June 11, 1785 and arrived on August 19, 1785 after 69 days at sea.

Le Saint Remi: The fourth ship left on Thursday, June 27, 1785 and arrived on September 10, 1785 after 75 days at sea.

L'Amitie: The fifth ship left France on August 20,1785 and arrived on November 8, 1785 after 80 days.

La Ville d'Archangel: The sixth ship that left France on August 12, 1785 and arrived in Louisiana on December 3, 1785 after 113 days ashore. Ran aground on November 4, and they had already run out of food. The trip saw 15 deaths and 2 desertions. Fifty-three families decided to go to Bayoudes Ecores, North of Baton Rouge, Louisiana. After a hurricane aboute ten years later, settlers moved south to join the other Acadians in Lafourche area.

La Caroline: The seventh and final ship left France on October

9, 1785 and reached Louisiana on December 7, 1785 after 54 days at sea.

The first six ships left from Nantes, France which is also know as Paimbouef. The Archangel left from St. Malo, France. All ships arrived in New Orleans, some earlier than others. Many lives did not make it. Limited research proved that all of my ancestors during the 1785 exodus did make it through the journey to Louisiana. However, the jouney in 1759 had a different outcome. A much more difficult and tragic result. Because of brutal and harsh conditions of the long jouney, I find that one of my ancestors did not make it to the new world. My heart sunk when my research for one of my ancestors ended in a terrible tragedy.

Chapter 7
Buried At Sea

Generation 7
1697-1759
Francois Chiasson 1697
Anne Doucet Chiasson 1703-buried at sea 1759

In 1749, during the departation, over 2000 settlers were brought to Acadia by the English. In 1755 the departation of Acadians began with over 6000 being exiled. Many were sent to France or Louisiana. The territory controlled by France, the British round up in Nova Scotia took place in the fall of 1755. British captured the French fortress at Louisbourg in July of 1758. They rounded up most of the Acadians in Ile Royale and on Ile St. Jean. Later that year the British packed hundreds of Acadians into vessels that were originally used for hired merchants and deported them to St. Malo and other French ports. The ship, Duke Williams left Ile Royale in August and did not reach St. Malo until early November. This ship suffered an explosion during a middle Atlantic storm. Acadian Joseph Doucet believed to be Ann Doucet's brother reached St. Malo in 1759. Ann Doucet, my fifth Great Grand Mother, her husband, Francois Chiasson and two of their youngest sons, Chrysostome and Louis crossed over on one of the five British transports believed to be The Archangel. They reached St. Malo, France in late January of 1759. Anne never made it there alive. Anne, our fifth Great

Grand Mother was buried at sea.

Our fifth Great Grand Father, Francois Chiasson was born in 1697 in Beaubassin, Acadia. He was christened at St. Anne Church in Beaubassin, Nova Scotia. His Father was Gabriel Chiasson and his Mother was Marie Savoie, both born in Acadia. Francois was a ploughman and a fisherman. When Francois was about twenty-five years of age he married Anne Doucet on November 3, 1722 in Port Royal, Nova Scotia. Our fifth Great Grand Mother, Anne was about nineteen years of age. Together they had nine children. Jean Baptiste, our fourth Great Grand Father was the elder. They also had Francois Chiasson, born in about 1729 in Acadia. Joseph Chiasson was born May 8, 1733 in Isle of Jean. Anne was born on March 25, 1736. Josephe Marie was born on November 1, 1738. Marie was born about the year of 1740. Louis was born on April 18, 1741. Louise Felicite was born December 20, 1743. The ninth child, Chrysostome was born about in 1747.

Our fifth Great Grand Father, Francois barely survived the journey but died nearly one month after reaching his destination on February 14, 1759 in St. Servan, Ille at Vilaine, France. He was buried two days later. The harsh conditions of the journey took its toll on our family. The ship left in August and arived in late January 1759. The conditions were brutal and it cost our family a huge sacrifice, the precious life of our fifth Great Grand Mother.

Chapter 8
Scattered Abroad

Generation 8
1667-1741
Gabriel (Dit Pierre) Chiasson 1667-4/10/1741
Marie Savoie Chiasson 1669

As our tree stand in the mist of the forest I can not help but to see that life has its harsh realities. Our leaves were as a green and flattened structure sitting softly upon our main branch of our family tree. Attached to the stym, we function as a principal organ creating lives. Our leaf like structure awaits new life and many challenges come with new beginnings. A difficult life it must have been, a simplistic kind of life that was less complicated. A life where days were filled with working in the gardens, washing clothes with a wash board, baking and rising of the bread, sewing and making clothes by hand and living the simple life that in most places have never existed or no longer exists.

Port Royal in Nova Scotia was one of the first areas that were settled. In 1636 the ship, St. Jehan arrived with my ancestors and others soon followed it.

Our sixth Great Grand Father, Gabriel Chiasson was born in 1667 in Beaubassin, Acadia. His original name was Gabriel Dit Pierre Chiasson, given name Gabriel. Back in France they used the term Dit, the meaning in our language is AKA which is "As Known As". His Father was Guyon Chiasson and his Mother, Jeanne Bernard. He married my sixth Great Grand Mother, Marie Savoie in about 1688 in Port Royal, Acadia. Marie was born on or around May 1670. She was the daughter of Francois Savoie and Catherine Lejeune at Beaubassin. In 1686 Gabriel served as a Domestic in the household of Chignecto Seigneur, Michel Leneuf de La Valliere. Michel was born in 1640 and died in 1705 and he had four sons. He was a military figure who became the Governor of Acadia under French control. The Leneuf family came from Caen, France and settled in Trois-Rivierer, Quebec. He was the first noble to settle in New France and help a high position of power and prestige through several generations. Gabriel was a skilled servant whose work encompassed many skills and management tasks in the Governor's mansion. In March of 2008, the ILO Governing Body brought into affect decent work for domestic workers and on the agenda of the ninety ninth Session of the International Labour Conference of 2010 they set labour standards. Past conditions that were faced by domestic workers have changed in the last centuries. There has been more movements going forth for the labour rights, immigrnat rights and many conditions were changed where domestic workers are now protected. In 2011 the International Labour Organization adopted the Convention Concerning descent work for domestic workers. Gabriel worked both inside and outside of the mansion for many years and was very loyal to his employer.
Gabriel was twenty-six years old when he married Marie.

Together, they had ten but possibly eleven children and all were born in Beaubassin, Acadia. The eldest, Michel Chiasson was born in 1689. It is believed that Michel also worked for the Governor, Michell Le Neuf de La Valliere, of the valley. Pierre Chiasson was born in 1691. Jean Baptiste was born in 1692. Marie Joseph was born in 1694. Francois Chiasson, my fifth Great Grand Father and the family tree line was born in 1697. Abraham was born in about 1700. Francoise was born in about 1701. Anne was born in 1708. Marguerite was born in about 1710 and Judith Chiasson was born in about 1713.

When our sixth Great Grand Father, Gabriel was born , at that time according to the censuses, in 1670 The Treaty of Breda in 1667 returned Acadia to France. The new French governor Grandfontaine brought 30 soldiers and 60 settlers with him. His job was to restore French authority. Acadia was in between two colonies, New France and New England, therefore it was always under attack. It did not receive a lot of help from France. The Acadians taught themselves how to make and repair material needed to survive. They also used the barter system with the New Englanders when they could not get or make new items. This type of trading was not allowed.
The first census was in 1671 when Grandfontaine arrived and it gives a record of the earliest Acadian people. The 1671 Census reported 392 people, but some were not counted. Most of them were in Port Royal and areas around Acadia. Esitmates populate the numbers as high as 500.
In 1678 another census was taken. It listed parents, children but no names and age of the children. It also listed their livestock. In 1684 Governorship was Francois Marie Perrot. He portrayed the Acadians as living a simple and pastoral life. They were self

sufficient, hard working who never lacked in meat or bread. But they would never save by putting away any harvest in case they had a bad year. In 1686 there were 57 people, 10 families, 83 acres tilled, 90 cattle, 21 sheep, 67 pigs and 20 guns.
In 1686 another census was done. In 1688 there was a shortage of manure to develope the uplands. The shortage of labor and tidelands was the reason that 25-30 people had moved to Minas. Most of them were younger people.

Our sixth Great Grand Father, Gabriel, died on April 10, 1741 at the age of 75 and was buried on April 11, 1741 His wife, our sixth Great Grand Mother, Marie died on or before 1714. Gabriel (dit Pierre) Chiasson is listed as a widower in 1714.

List of Ships from France to Louisiana

Le Phillippe- La Rochelle France to Louisina January 25, 1719
Le St. Louis (The St. Louis)- May 28, 1719
The Marie-May 28, 1719
The Union- May 28, 1719
Les Deux Feres (Two Brothers) 1719
Le Marechal d'Estrees- August 19, 1719
Le Duc de Noailles- September 16, 1719
La Duchesse de Noailles- 1719, From Louisiana to La Rochelle France.

In 1749 over 2000 settlers were brought to Acadia from the English. In 1755 the deportation of Acadians began. Over 6000

Acadians were exiled and sent to France and Louisiana. The Acadians withstood the test of times. Their love for their family was strong and their leaves were for the healing of the nations. Our leaves were scattered abroad the nations setting our ancestors on our path and our journey that would take us out of one country and into another world, another time and another life.

Chapter 9

Reproduction- Offsprings

1640-1693
Generation 9
Guyon "Denis, Dion" Chiasson (aka Giasson, dit Lavallee)-
1640-1693
Marriage 1 Jeanne Bernard Chiasson 1643-1680's
Marriage 2 Marie Belliveau-1655-after 1680Marie
Marriage 3 Madeleine Martin Chiasson 1666-about
1684

As each generation reproduces and spread abroad our family tree, we come to increase greatly. I try to imagine original images of our generations. Our ancestors multiplying and reproducing our relatives. Each generation living out their lives as planned by God. Setting the course for each generation to imitate. One generation carries out their course in life followed by other generations to come.

As I am writing, a loud sound of the horn coming from the mail man, as she warns me that I have a package and mail to pick up. I can not help to think back in the 1600's where there was no mail man. Layers of generations that lived according to the times of their lives. One generation using horse and buggy while older generations use glass bottles for all information, census and government information reports that were documented. They would then dig a hole in the ground and place the bottle for safe keep. The ground was also considered their banks, keeping all of their money and important items. This is how they did their census and how we are able to know some critical information of how they lived back then.

Our seventh Great Grand Father, Guyon Chiasson, also know as Denis, Dion aka giasson dit Lavallee was born in or about 1638 in La Rochelle, France. He was christened in La Rochelle, Haute Saone at St. Nicolas Church in France. He was a Farmer. His Father was Pierre Chiasson born about 1620 in France and Marie Peroche born about 1622 also in France. Guyon married Jeanne Bernard. She was born between 1646-1647in Port Royal, Acadia. She was christened in Nova Scotia at St. Jean Baptist,canada. She was the daughter of Bernard and Andree. They were married in 1666 in Port Royal, Acadia. Together they had eight children. Gabriel, my 6th Great Grand Father is the eldest. Marie Chiasson was born in 1667. Jean was born in 1668. Francois Chiasson was born in 1668. Sebastien Chiasson was born in 1670 and Michel Chiasson was born in 1675 and before October 7, 1683. All of the children were born in Beaubassin, Acadia. Not all eight children are counted for. Jeanne died after 1675 and Guyon married his second wife Marie Belliveau on about 1677, in Beaubassin, New Brunswick at St. Anne's in Canada. Together they birthed Anne Chiasson born in 1680 in Beaubassin, Acadia. Jeannne died after 1680 and Guyon married his third wife Marie Madeleine Martin on October 7, 1683 at the age of forty-two. Marie was born on June 29, 1666 in Quebec, Canada. Marie Madeleine is the daughter of Pierre Martin of

Sillery. Together, they birthed five children. One set of twins, Angelique and Marguerite, born in 1684. Genevieve was born in 1685. Marie was born in 1691 and Anne Chiasson was born in 1692. All of the children were born in Beaubassin, Acadia. Guyon died on April 10, 1741 in Beaubassin, Nova Scotia and is buried at St. Anne Cemetary in Canada. One of Guyon's daughters moved to Ile St. Jean, today called Prince Edward Island, by 1720's and was among the earliest European settlers on the island.

Guyon may have inscribed himself into the military regiment at some point because in the census of 1686 he is listed under the surename, Lavalee. A French soldiers custom is for a French soldier to take a nom de guerre, french for an assumed name, as one under which a person fights. Many continued to use their assumed names after they left the military. After 1686 Guyon was one of the most prosperous residence of Beaubassen with forty arpents of land under cultivation. It is believed that Guyon had a total of fourteen children leaving ancestors all over Acadia and eventually Louisiana. Guyon died around 1693 in his middle 50's in Beaubassin, Nova Scotia, Acadia, Canada. He is burried at St. Anne Cemetary, Canada.

Chapter 10
Planting of the Seeds

Generation 10
1614-1657
Pierre Chiasson (aka Giasson) 1614-1657
Marie Madeleine Peroche-1622-

Seeds are defined as a mature plant ovule containing an embryo enclosed in a protective outer covering. As each generation is uncovered from their protective covering I find seeds spread abroad in a nation that I knew nothing of.

Our eighth Great Grand Father and tenth generation, Pierre Chiasson, also known as Giasson was born about 1620 in La Rochelle, France. His Father is Robert Chiasson born between 1585-1596. No report or research was found at this time of his Mother. He married Marie Madeleine Peroche in about the year of 1639 in La Rochelle, France. Marie was born in about 1622 in La Rochelle, France. Together, they had five children, Marie, Louise, Jeanne, Francois and Guyon Chiasson. Guyon was my direct line of descendants and was bron in 1638 in France. Pierre was a Farmer, Ploughman and a Laborer and his Domicillie A La rochelle, France. Pierre died on October 7, 1657.

As each generation is researched I found that it got a little harder to locate family information. We are so blessed to have found out any kind of information on our ancestors. The more I seek into our Family Tree, i find out more information into the lives of our ancestors. The seeds that were planted long ago still exist today. Our family tree has blossomed from this tiny mustard seed, a tiny acorn and has multiplyed on the earth today. Our Family Tree has made me who I am today. As I study, I find more interesting details and as I seek it, I find more wisdom. It's in comparison to the word of God, we all have faith as a tiny mustard seed. When we take the seed of faith and spread it abroad, we release the hope for our families, our friends and the nation. A seed, capable of producing life. When we cast a good seed out, it will come back to us. When it does it will be multiplyed, some thirty, some sixty and some even a hundred. Have you casted your good seed today?

Chapter 11
The True Vine

1585
Generation 11
Robert Chiasson

Robert Chiasson was born in 1585 and he is our ninth Great Grand Father. Through much research I could not find my ninth Great Grand Mother's name and information. She did give birth to Pierre on about 1614. Research places her birth in the time of early 1590's. Robert was twenty-nine years of age when they had Pierre.

As my research start to take me to a closure and less information was to be found, it saddened me to come almost to the end of my journey in locating my ancestors. I wanted to find out more and if I searched more I probably could find more. I realize how important it is for each generation to record their immediate family. In doing this we can see the whole tree of our family. When I started out in search for my family it was as a puzzle with bits and pieces coming to the light one search at a time. Many years have passed since I started the long search and I see some things in a spiritual mind. God truly is the vine and we are the branches for without him we can do nothing. By the grace of God he has placed my feet upon this path of slopes and mountains. In the words of a parable, with God and by faith, we truly can see the forest behind the tree. The forest meaning God who is the true spreading vine and the tree meaning our family.

Chapter 12
Forest Behind The Trees

1560-
Generation 12
Cyril Chaisson 1560
Barbara Connors Chaisson 1565

As we enter our twelth generation of our Family Tree, our eyes
are set on the huge forest behind our Family Tree. My research
on our family covers a large area of many ancestors and
generations. The journey has taken me back as early as 1560.
Our colorful tree has spread our roots across this beautiful land.
I thank God that my ancestors sailed from France to Louisiana.
The Bayou State, Sportsman Paradise and The Pelican State
always calls out to me whenever we are on a journey. I am so
thankful and honored to be called a Cajun. Acadians had been
different and unique people since the beginning and I believe
God wanted us that way. He set us apart and seperated us. He
saved us for his glory. It was not very hard to locate the
generations because we simply stayed put and lived a quiet and
peaceful life. Our hands were busy at creating and working hard.
Family was important to us as I uncovered generations of large
families that stuck by each other.

Our twelfth generation and tenth Great Grand Father, Cyril Chiasson was born about 1560 in France. He married our tenth Great Grand Mother Babara Connors Chiasson who was born about 1565. When Cyril was twenty-five years of age and Babara was about twenty, Robert was born.

This brings me to the end of my long journey in search for my ancestors. The longing to know more about my ancestors constantly reminds me that knowledge and wisdom is a gift from God. We must seek out information and cherish what we find. I hold my family very dear to my heart. Besides God, it is the most important thing to me.

Many families are a part of our tree and tie in through marriage. Many different last names are involved and intertwine into our tree. It is your job to search out your family name to find your hidden treasures.

Chapter 13
Closing
A Tree Standing Strong,
In A Place That We Call Home

The puzzle of our lives and location of our families come together not in closing but to a temporary halt. At times it seemed our family was a jungle spread abroad as a wild fire. The research is endless and if I would have continued to look for more information I believe that I would have found so much more. In 1985 when I first started researching, my search ended in Thibodaux before my Great Grand Fathers and Great Grand Mothers left France. I would have had to go to France for more information but today we are able to find so much more through technology. Often times I could almost see one of my Great Grand Mothers washing clothes with home made soap and a wash board. I think about my relatives playing as children on home made boards used as see saws. Horses and mules as the main transportation and work tools. It would have been a treasure just to hear some of the stories that I had been told come to life as I watch it unfold with my own eyes. What would I give to watch my Daddy make his boys hand sewn suits as he did when he was alive. To see my Mother rocking my younger brothers. Watch my ancestors of past generations work with their hands and make their own boats and houses. I pray one day we can all be together to meet each of the ancestors that we never met on earth. To trade stories about our special time that God gave us here on this earth. To spend time again with limitless time as brothers and sisters in heaven and to dwell in the midst of the Garden and the Tree of Life. To walk on golden paved streets and communicate with our loved ones. To live eternally with Jesus and all of the saints in the bible. What a beautiful place it will be. God has been so good to us by providing a family that did the best and worked hard all of their lives for us. Although each generation had their challenges we proved to be overcomers. We proved that we were more than conquerers through Christ Jesus. Our family is blessed and not cursed. My children have over fourteen generations to treasure. My grand children have a legacy of over fifteen generations. I have no grand children married yet but when they do, their children can now account for sixteen generations. What an awesome accomplishment and a testimony of the faith, hope and love of a family. Blessings do not only show up in money but in the gift of knowledge, wisdom and the treasures of a wonderful family. Our family, a tree of life standing in the midst of the forest. A gift from God given to us long ago before we were ever born.

Revelation2:7 He that has an ear, let him hear what the Spirit of says unto the churches; To him that overcometh will I give to eat of the tree of life, which is in the midst of the paradise of God. God has always made available for us the tree of life. Our decisions and choices always chose the tree of knowledge between good and evil, choosing evil. Our face constantly turns toward evil every time. Seduced, deceived and beguiled each time by the devil, we become ashamed of the wrong consequences for the decisions we have made in our lives. We become naked and forced to hide ourselves with fig leaves. Consumed with our own guilt and shame of the things we have done in our inmature state of mind. In Christ, there is no shame. He has spread our sins as far as the east is to the west. Thrown in the sea of forgiveness and the lake of fire, our sins are washed away forever. It is our on self that brings it back up again. We pick it up daily and repeat the very thing that God has delivered and freed up from. Why do we continue to do this? Why do we sin more than we do righteous? Our flesh is an enemy to God and to our own selves. Flesh is contrary to our Spirit, God's Spirit. Our flesh carries sin and our Spirit carries life. Two entities warring at each other at all times. Our flesh is not capable of doing what is right on our own, not capable of doing good or just. For this reason, we should cast down every high thing that exalts itself against the knowledge of God. Cast down every imagination that is evil and contrary to the word of God. Easier said than done when our flesh desires the very thing that will destroy us. The thing we feed the most will have an incredible appetite that will exalt us or weigh us down. Our fleshly appetite will never be full, desiring to be fed and satisfied over and over again. The one we feed the most will be in control, will be stronger and will have it's authority in our lives.

Revelation 22:14 Blessed are they that do his comandments, that they may have right to the tree of life, and may enter through the gates into the city. We have the right to the tree of life and enter into the city when we live a righteous life. It is our inheritance as servants of God. We can go through the gates and enter into the tree of life and live in the freedom that we rightfully own and deserve. We are the branches and we live in the vine. Jesus is the vine that holds us up. God knows how long we have here on this earth for he has given us the length of time. He has ordained our first and our last breath. We may think that we are producing fruit all on our own strengths and abilities but without life and breath in us coming from the vine which is placed in us by God, we would not be living.

John 15:5 I am the vine, you are the branches. He that abides in me and I in him, the same brings forth much fruit: For without me you can do nothing.

"We are the branches". We are a family and God gave us our families. Our families could also mean the relationship with others. Families stick together, our sisters and our brothers in every circumstance no matter what storms of life comes our way. In love and unity for all eternity. There is no place like home when we are running wild and free. Our families take us back and embrace us once again. When we turn our face toward heaven, we will see our family. I can look back and see how my Father and Mother tried their best to raise our family and make a home even as our branches shook violently in the storms of life. They showed us how to be a great example to live by and the determination and strength to never give up. How they taught us not to be busy bodies but to be hard working. God made our families so we could have a strong pillar to lean against when we are week. We are a family of God that brings forth much fruit and God has truly blessed us and our families.

Our family, as a tree standing tall in the midst of the forest.

Spreading like wild fires and its flames shed abroad. We represent a light in this world and a city on a hill. When we shine our light we will see the break of dawn. When you find you have lost your way and can not get through another day, hold on to the break of dawn for it is in plain sight. You might feel that you can not rely on your family, if this is so then rely on God. He is there and when we pray he can change our families but the change must first come from us. Though the sorrow may last for a night, joy will always comes in the morning. When we choose to hold on tight our faith, hope and love will hold us until the break of dawn. Look for the break of dawn. It is on the horizon!

Luke 21:29 And he spoke to them a parable; Behold the fig tree, and all the trees; (30) When they now shoot forth, ye see and know of your selves that summer is now nigh at hand. (31) so likewise you, when you see that the kingdom of God is nigh at hand. (32) Verily I say unto you, This generation shall not pass away, till all be fulfilled. (33) Heaven and Earth shall pass away: but my words shall not pass away. (34) And take heed to yourselves, lest at any time your hearts be overcharged with surfeiting, and drunkenness, and cares of this life, and so that day come upon you unawares. (35) For as a snare shall it come on all them that dwell on the face of the whole earth. (36) Watch you therefore, and pray always, that ye may be accounted worthy to escape all these things that shall come to pass, and to stand before the Son of man. When the buds show forth her sign by shooting out, a new and fresh season is on it's way. God shows signs of each change of seasons and we must stay on full alert. If we are asleep when we should be working, we will miss the blessings.

Embrace your family because time is short here on this earth. We have a certain amount of time to get the things done that God expects of us. Embrace forgiveness because grudges lerk in dark places and breed lonliness, revenge, bitterness and jealousy. So the song goes, Let It Go! Turn Around And Slam The Door! Have no part of unforgiveness. Cast a good fruit by being a peace maker. Live life unselfishly by helping others in need. Comfort others when they mourn. Stay away from drama but pray for those who are week. Help those who are in need when it is in your power to do it. Visit the sick and let them know you care. Tend to the orphans and help them as much as possible. Spend time listening to widows and widowers. All they need is for someone to listen and know that we care. They want someone to hear them when they reminisce old times. We are all living life with our branches hook to the vine and passing through this life while spreading abroad new life to the whole earth. Our roots are planted strong to an unreachable depth within the foundation of this earth. Our barks are guiding and directing our footsteps in a righteous direction. Our shoots sprouting out and extending ourtward to unreachable height. We are all planting and laboring together in this peculiar place that we call home, this earth and our lives, to produce this gigantic "Family Tree".

We are a Family! As a tree standing strong, in a place that we call home. God Bless Our Family!

Resources used for the creating of
"We Are The Branches"

King James Bible
Rootsweb.com, Ancestry.com
Vital Records, Family Documents, Family Bibles compiled by
M.L. Artigues.
Archives.com, World Connect.com
Wiki tree.com,
Community Family Tree.com,
Family Researchers,
William Cates
Google.com
Histoire et Genealogie Des Acadien; Volume #3,
Author Bona Arsenault

Author Whitney Dartez
The Dem Daily
Project Louisiana Acadian/Cajun
1880 United States Federal Census
World Connect Program, GEDCOM.
Researchers
Family
Friends

About The Author
Anna C. Bradford

A license and ordained Minister since 1999. Her and Michael
are Founders of Faith Ministries, International. A multi culture,
multi ministries and a non profit organization, a charity for
children.
With a desire to work with children in the early childhood
developement stages, she started up and directed prep-schools,
daycares and learning centers. Working along side of her
husband Mike as Missionaries to the borders of United States,
Mexico, South and Central America. Supporting and supplying
orphanages locally and international. Creating many children's
outreaches, school supply give aways and work projects for the
needy children in many areas.

Faith Without Works Is Dead!

Author of "At The Border", "Chasing After Butterflies", "A Child's Journey", "A Beautiful Garden", "How To Start Up And Run A Profitable Child Care Center". "The Acadians, Cajun Cook Book" and "The Acadians, Low Carb Cajun Cook Book". Her hobbies include gardening, baking, canning, sewing, motorcycle riding, fishing, shooting, keyboard, composing, singing and writing songs . She loves life, spending time with her family and sharing the gospel.

Purpose For This Book:

A deep hunger to know my ancestors became a driving force to do more research on my Chaisson Family Tree. One of my cousins started this tree around 1985 and it became a desire to search even deeper into the lives and the generations of my ancestors. Upon doing this I became fascinated by my findings. Everyone should have a hunger and a desire to find out where they came from and who their ancestors are. It will lead you into your journey and your identity as you search for your family. For this reason I have composed my families real life stories into this book and titled it
"We Are The Branches".

Made in the USA
Columbia, SC
30 July 2024

39140981R00037